# What's Inside a
# Fire Truck?

# ¿Qué hay dentro de un
# camión de bomberos?

## Sharon Gordon

Marshall Cavendish
Benchmark
New York

# Inside a Fire Truck
## Dentro de un camión de bomberos

| | | | | |
|---|---|---|---|---|
| **1** | air tanks<br>tanques de oxígeno | | **5** | fire extinguisher<br>extintor de incendios |
| **2** | aerial ladder<br>escalera telescópica | | **6** | light cable<br>cable de electricidad |
| **3** | axes<br>hachas | | **7** | lights<br>reflectores |
| **4** | covers<br>lonas | | **8** | outriggers<br>balancines |

| # | English | Spanish |
|---|---------|---------|
| 9 | pike poles | picas |
| 10 | rescue basket | camilla de canasta |
| 11 | saw blades | sierras |
| 12 | siren | sirena |
| 13 | toolboxes | cajas de herramientas |
| 14 | turnout gear | equipo de asistencia |
| 15 | venting fans | ventiladores |
| 16 | water cooler | recipiente de agua |

Watch out! The fire truck is coming.

The firefighters switch on the *siren* and the emergency lights. The lights flash and turn.

---

¡Cuidado! Ahí viene el camión de bomberos.

Los bomberos prenden la *sirena* y las luces de emergencia, que giran y son intermitentes.

Two firefighters sit inside the front cab. Four or five more sit behind them.

The *dispatcher* gives the address over the radio. The fire chief works out a plan to fight the fire.

❖

Dos bomberos van sentados en la cabina delantera. Cuatro o cinco más van sentados atrás.

El *operador* da la dirección por el radio, y el jefe de bomberos hace planes para combatir el fuego.

Firefighters use yellow tape to mark the fire line. It keeps people away from the fire.

❖

Los bomberos usan una cinta amarilla para marcar la zona de peligro y mantener a la gente alejada del fuego.

The ladder truck goes to work first.

The tall *aerial ladder* rises into the sky. The *outriggers* keep the truck steady.

❖

El camión escalera es el primero en salir.

La alta *escalera telescópica* se eleva hacia el cielo mientras los *balancines* mantienen firme al camión.

The aerial ladder can reach people trapped in high places.

A firefighter also can stand on the ladder with his hose. He sprays water or special chemicals onto the fire.

❖

La escalera telescópica puede llegar a sitios altos donde hay gente atrapada.

Un bombero también puede pararse en la escalera con la manguera y regar agua o químicos especiales contra el fuego.

Smaller ladders are kept on the sides of the truck.
A first-aid kit is inside the truck, too.

❖

Las escaleras más pequeñas se guardan a los
lados del camión, y dentro, el botiquín de primeros
auxilios.

Many firefighters are paramedics. The *paramedics* use the kit to help people who are hurt.

---❖---

Muchos bomberos son *paramédicos*. Los paramédicos usan el botiquín para ayudar a los heridos.

Inside the truck, there are hooks, axes, and poles. They are used to break down walls, doors, and windows.

Sometimes, firefighters make holes in rooftops. The holes let out smoke and heat.

---

En el camión hay ganchos, hachas y picas. Los usan para derribar paredes, puertas y ventanas.

A veces, los bomberos hacen huecos en los techos para dejar salir el humo y el calor.

When everyone is safe, the pumper truck gets to work. The pumper can use water from its own tank, or it can hook up to a *fire hydrant*.

❖

Cuando todos están a salvo, el camión de bombeo empieza a trabajar. El camión de bombeo puede usar el agua de su tanque o puede conectarse a un *hidrante*.

A big hose connects to the truck. It carries water from the hydrant into the pumper.

❖

La manguera grande se conecta al camión y lleva el agua del hidrante al camión de bombeo.

Long rows of flat hoses are folded on top of the truck.

❖

Las hileras largas de mangueras planas están dobladas sobre el camión.

The firefighters aim the hose at the fire. The truck pumps water through the hose. The jet of water can be as long as a football field.

❖

Los bomberos apuntan la manguera al fuego y el camión bombea agua por la manguera. El chorro de agua puede ser tan largo como una cancha de fútbol americano.

The truck's control panel shows the water pressure. If the pressure is too high, the hose can get out of control. If it is too low, the water will not reach the fire.

---

El tablero de mandos del camión muestra la presión del agua. Si la presión es muy alta, la manguera puede salirse de control. Si es muy baja, el agua no llega hasta el fuego.

The pumper has many other firefighting tools.
A *fire extinguisher* can put out small fires.

❖

El camión de bombeo tiene muchas otras
herramientas antiincendios. Un *extintor de
incendios* puede apagar fuegos pequeños.

Air tanks and masks help the firefighters breathe through the smoke.

❖

Las máscaras y los tanques de oxígeno ayudan a los bomberos a respirar a través del humo.

When the fire is out, the trucks return to the firehouse. The firefighters check and clean their equipment. The trucks are washed and polished.

The firefighters need a good scrubbing, too!

---

Cuando el fuego está apagado, los camiones regresan al cuartel de bomberos. Los bomberos revisan y limpian el equipo. Lavan y lustran los camiones.

¡Los bomberos también necesitan una buena limpieza!

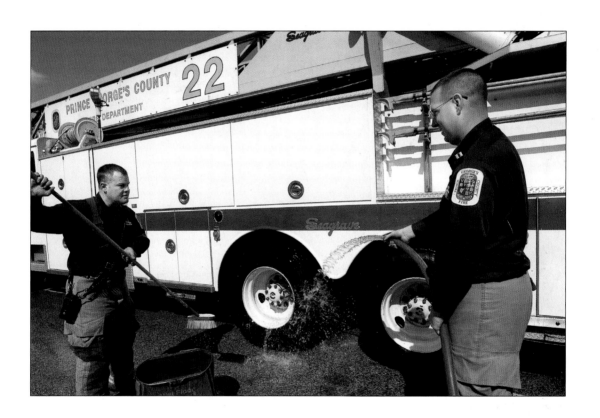

# Challenge Words

**aerial ladder** A very tall ladder that can reach the tops of high buildings.

**dispatcher** A phone operator who takes emergency calls for the police, ambulance, and fire stations.

**fire extinguisher** A red cylinder that contains firefighting liquid or powder.

**fire hydrant** A metal pipe on the edge of a sidewalk that is connected to the main water supply.

**outriggers** Strong metal legs that brace the fire truck and hold it steady.

**paramedic** A person trained to treat injured and sick people.

**siren** An electrical horn that makes a loud up-and-down warning sound.

# Palabras avanzadas

**balancines** Unas fuertes patas de metal que sostienen el camión de bomberos y lo mantienen firme.

**escalera telescópica** Una escalera que está sobre el camión de bomberos y que puede alcanzar la cima de los edificios altos.

**extintor de incendios** Un cilindro rojo que contiene líquido o polvo para apagar el fuego.

**hidrante** Una tubería de metal en el borde de la acera que está conectada al suministro de agua.

**operador(a)** Una persona que recibe las llamadas de emergencia para la policía, ambulancias y estaciones de bomberos.

**paramédico(a)** Una persona entrenada para atender a los heridos y enfermos.

**sirena** Una bocina eléctrica que hace un sonido fuerte de alerta, agudo y grave.

# Index

Page numbers in **boldface** are illustrations.

# Índice

Las páginas indicadas con números en **negrita** tienen ilustraciones.

With thanks to Nanci Vargus, Ed.D.
and Beth Walker Gambro, reading consultants

ACKNOWLEDGMENTS
With thanks to Chief Michael Rau, Midland Park Fire Department,
Midland Park, New Jersey, the Prince George's County Fire
Department, and the men and women of the Tuxedo-Cheverly Station

Marshall Cavendish Benchmark
99 White Plains Road
Tarrytown, New York 10591-9001
www.marshallcavendish.us

Library of Congress Cataloging-in-Publication Data

Gordon, Sharon.
[What's inside a fire truck? Spanish & English]
Whats inside a fire truck? = ¿Qué hay dentro de un camión de bomberos? / Sharon Gordon. — Bilingual ed.
p. cm. — (Bookworks, what's inside? = ¿Qué hay dentro?)
Includes index.
ISBN-13: 978-0-7614-2472-7 (bilingual edition)
ISBN-10: 0-7614-2472-5 (bilingual edition)
ISBN-13: 978-0-7614-2391-1 (Spanish edition)
ISBN-10: 0-7614-1563-7 (English edition)
1. Fire engines—Juvenile literature. 2. Fire extinction—Juvenile literature. I. Title.
II. Title: ¿Qué hay dentro de un camión de bomberos? III. Series.

TH9372.G67318 2007
628.9'259—dc22
2006018911

Spanish Translation and Text Composition by Victory Productions, Inc.
www.victoryprd.com

Photo Research by Anne Burns Images

Cover Photo by Jay Mallin

The photographs in this book are used with permission and through the courtesy of: *Jay Mallin*:
pp. 1, 2, 3, 5, 6, 9, 11, 14, 15, 17, 18, 20, 21, 22, 24, 26, 27, 29. *Corbis*: p. 13 Kim Kulish.

Series design by Becky Terhune

Printed in Malaysia
1  3  5  6  4  2